Mysterious Existence

Lynne Zotalis

skeleton tree exposé

All truly wise thoughts have been thought already thousands of times; but to make them really ours we must think them over again honestly, till they take firm root in our personal experience. Goethe

Published by Human Error Publishing

www.humanerrorpublishing.com
paul@humanerrorpublishing.com

ISBN: 978-1-948521-04-8

Cover design
Cover photo: Lynne Zotalis
Human Error Publishing

Contents

Land of My Heart 9

Silken Haze 10

Pandemic Paroxysm 11

It's None of Your Fucking Business 13

My New Job or Mission of Mercy 14

We Are One Family 16

Puzzle Zen 18

Ruins 20

Passage of Years 22

Quantified Love 23

Advice 24

When I First Loved You 26

Moonglow 28

Does Time Heal All? 29

My Life 32

Sacred Remnants 34

On Tenterhooks 35

Defensible Space 36

A Singular Drive... 285 37

Cross My Heart 38

Serenity 40

Fix 41

Talk To Me 42

Christmas Lost 43

Hey, What Doesn't Kill You 45

Who Let Go? 46

Glorious Rain 47

Sojourner 49

So Lost 51

Always Reaching 53

Angst 54

Me Too Mother 55

Dawn Into Dusk 57

What Matters? 60

Delight Song 61

Mother Nature Killer Beeaach   63
Dear Diary   64
AKA Yeti   65
I Have No Defense   66
Ersatz Liaison (Unplugged)   67
Remember loneliness   68
Circle of Belonging   70
Fly, My Lovelies   71
Perennial Life   72
Itsy Bitsy Spider   74
Pragmatist   75
I Thought This Would Last Forever   76
Is All Love Schizo?   77
A Life in Process   78

streaks of dawn's decoration

Land of my Heart

This sky is très spectaculaire
as I lie on the slate stone courtyard
astral planing
amongst lucent clouds revealing a canvas,
contrails accentuating
gossamer wisps, vapor haze
fusing white with azure gray,
innuendo of coral.

Ahhh…
my breath makes the sound of longing,
stay forever, cradle me within your tranquil spell,
entrancing me till I blush crimson.
Fuse me
with the vision I can witness
only this once, this singular twilight.
My eyes reflect the waning sunlight, still
with soul-penetrating rays, warming from inside out
these somnolent bones—
a surreal gift this clement evening, autumn
in my enchanted land.

Silken Haze

it's all
about choices,
which voices
will I heed,
how I decide
to abide
in peace,
in gratitude,
unshackle
what is bound
underground
gloved
in heart's alcove
of love
every day,
while we
display and convey
every hour,
in power
the struggle
to rise up
I
will
evolve
I
will
solve
the hazy
confusion
that permeates
days
and plays against
the shadow
to know
myself

Pandemic Paroxysm or HiderNation

I hate the mask   but
maybe that's too strong, okay, but I certainly don't like it
forgetting it,   STILL,   my safety net
realizing halfway across the parking lot,
turning around to retrieve it
medieval Latin— masca   translates to specter, nightmare
Arabic— maskharah, translates to buffoon, to ridicule,
and be mocked
it signifies something wrong
it relegates me to a hospital setting   as if I'm sick
untouchable Leper   stay away from me
don't approach more than 6 feet
don't hug me   my insecurity whispers you don't like me
you are afraid of me
I'm afraid of you
it's wrong
I don't even desire to go out because I'm so tired
of not seeing faces,
missing expressions, subtle suggestion,
I'd truly rather stay home than see everyone masked
angst saturation withers my soul,
it's wrong
so tired of virtual relationships
not a fan of zoom
we're all avoiding recognition like the KKK
protection of self, selfish, self-centered
I disguise my floundering mood,
covering and guarding personal space
it's wrong
gleaning visually through my soul's window
now restricted, barricaded in this cage of Covid trauma
learning disabled, unable to grasp the entire picture, idea
or perceive the suggestion of thought
in the absence of nuance or mere implication
trapped within this false front, a veneer,
where previously I used finesse

conveying thoughtfulness with pursed lips,
questioning by simply moving my mouth to one side,
sighing with open mouth exasperation,
biting my upper lip in dread
I'm having difficulty finding the words,
those specific idioms that layer communication
it's wrong
I do care about you and as long as I am able
will do everything I can to protect you
by compliance to scientific acuity
discounting my personal freedoms
demonstrating my capacity, my love
and compassion for humanity
donning the mask
for as long as it takes
as long as we are defined
by liberal, conservative, red and blue but
it is so wrong

It's None Of Your Fucking Business
(What's In My Wallet)

I have no patience with Wall Street,
intimidating investment brokers shaming me
for my short-sighted conservatism—
my money shouldn't be a chip
to be manipulated or influenced
by China's woes
or Greece's irresponsibility.
Who's responsible here?!
Only me.
I know exactly where every
dime of my meager savings is.
In a bank earning at best a whopping one percent.
Stagnant stagnation. Losing
due to inflation, the financial advisor's habitual harangue.
My confidence remains firm, resolved
to steer clear of that speculative black hole
of evaporative investing,
the game
persisting so long as
everyone, well, at least the key players,
keeps tossing around billions, even trillions
in monopoly money.

My New Job or Mission of Mercy

embarking on a mission of mercy to tend
the moribund parent, I entered the twilight zone,
a bubble filled with
tremendous wealth where charitable giving
is common at church but
homeless dare not venture (the Posse will get you)

not my chosen habitat but a requirement
maternal need
declining, no more fooling me--
decaying visage, twisted body
decrepit 90's, confused Swiss cheese memory
clinging to independence, facility
to appear eternally vibrant, ever in control, waning
but still able to admonish with age-old sanctions this
crumby, messy daughter
who will never measure up to impossible standards

I'm obliged to do my due diligence
manage the crises, the magic of LifeLine
propping one vertical
I won't shirk
hundred phone calls, please hold
maybe a call-back days later
home health-care interviews, ER, urology, GP
dozens of errands, My God! the errands

standing in line at CVS with Depends
"They're not for me!" I want to scream to noting eyes—
likely not the rain shower
depositing a puddle on the recliner
"Why do you do all this for me,"
gratefully she asks, "how do you?"
I hope someone will do it for me, I explain

(but I've made my daughter promise
to Kevorkian my ass
in lieu of diapers)

We Are One Family

The crisis at hand, on everyone's mind.
United in our anxiety, held together by faith and humanity.
You are my neighbor, you are my friend and I will do whatever I can
to keep you safe.
As well, I expect you to do the same for me.
I will wash my hands, I will not endanger myself or you.
What is in my power to do, I will.
This collective mind, our hidden or manifest fear
pulses like a drumbeat urging us to do more,
do something, anything.
We are sheltered in place, socially distanced, unable to touch, feel,
hug, kiss,
all of the comforting gestures that would calm us.
Those of us that can, that have a propensity to,   write.
Putting our thoughts and prayers,
our questions and confusion on paper
we attempt to move the frustrating elements
a minuscule distance away,
for a minute or possibly longer.
I am also of a mind to place blame,
even though I know that is generally not healthy
for the overall psyche
but it is needful for me to vent...
I hold 45, a presidunce,
the commandeerer in chief primarily responsible for the ignorance
and initial understatement of the covid pandemic
while he bloviated about his control over the virus.
Claiming it could not have been foreseen,
that testing was going smoothly hyperbolating
even self-aggrandizing throughout his public appearances
I shuddered at his ineptitude.
When pressed for answers to the rocketing situation he blamed
President Obama!
45's pandemic team abruptly left the administration.
They were not replaced.
The Centers for Disease Control were steadily defunded.

16

How does one tell if Rumpletrumpskin lies?
Hah! His mouth is moving!
He claimed people were being heavily tested
before allowed back in the United States
but there was only enhanced screening
not tests for COVID-19!
And this one, "more lives will be lost through suicide
if we don't lift the shelter in place sanction by Easter 2020!"
Outrageously irresponsible and ignorant false claims meant to
scare, intimidate and distract.
A million deaths… and counting
Wake up! Do not be duped.
Listen carefully and heed
as much as possible.
Be smart.
Be kind.
Be safe.

Puzzle Zen

During the pandemic I've done oh, probably a hundred jigsaw puzzles in an effort to stay sane, to clear my troubled, muddled mind. Outward appearance is a quick study and ... we can learn lessons anywhere, if we are open. From a puzzle? Why not? From the picture on the box I can determine if I'm going to like it or be able to finish it. I'm also a fairly good judge of character, in the initial meeting listening, assessing body language, direct eye contact. Not that I jump to conclusions but I have learned to trust my initial reaction and my inner voice.

At this age, a senior citizen, I do not have a lot of time for games or lies or Republicans. And like with the puzzle one has to be patient, sensing where something might work, a certain turn or twist might be fitting. Looking for the subtle alteration of hues, from grayish blue to hazy pink darkening to purple, lavender and cobalt. Barely perceptible you might notice a broadening concept, the landscape rising from calm seas to cloudless sky, where if you were on the opposite side you could see the alteration as you come at it from another angle finding the cohesion, the synergy it requires to be open minded enough to engage, to benefit the whole. But you have to observe and perceive, have the willingness to be tolerant or persistent, to catch the slight nuance. Can you find the commonality?

I am so stuck in my ideology, my convictions but I know rigidity and confrontation will not promote equanimity. Who responds to force? I certainly don't. You cannot jam those pieces into compliance mutilating the edge. Maybe it would fit if turned slightly, if looked at without preconceptions or a brighter light. You have to keep picking up another and another, a measured response. Is there a way to find the one that gently slides into that larger picture? I've given up on certain impossibly challenging puzzles, completely mystified by my inability to rationally solve the conundrum after laboring hours, days, and weeks tenaciously devoted to that end. Looking at the same pieces, over and over, trying the various combinations, loathe to admit defeat I cannot believe there isn't a way to logically achieve synergism. It is completely frustrating and baffling, this apparent divide an obvious failure. But almost as galling, even sad, is to get so far, nearing the final empty space to learn there is one missing. The discarded element, irrevocably lost.

Each time I dump the box of a thousand onto the table to begin the process I have to trust that the separated conglomerate of pieces will come together in the end. Is it faith? Is it hope? Allow me to elucidate; in a better future, the one that I envision and imagine, where harmony and kindness abide, I have this belief that every shape and color will paint the world with acceptance, respect, inclusion and grace. Dignity and teamwork will govern our actions, tolerance and honesty will align all factions and peace will rule the day. The puzzle has illuminated my perception with this analogous lesson thereby causing me to reassess my attitudes, the way I approach all of those in diverse boxes, to hear the way I am inflexible, how I am not without responsibility or culpability. I will endeavor to take a step back, take a deep breath and observe. We need each and every piece to complete the landscape.

Ruins

Time rusted, flayed under sun blazed days
Corroded metal, wood to shrunken hulls
Paint faded, chipped remnants of eras long gone
Preserved in museum form
Stirring images
Graveyard to junkyard
Remembrance inscribed
Walls desperate to remain
Gravity erasing
Brick by brick
Who lived here
Drove the dusty canvas
To lie down under red clay?
Frozen in time, the moment of release
Gave up the lingering ghost
To other worlds
Skeleton twisted
Incongruous slicing through
Horizon   the body, the shell, a façade wearing
Away for another century
As a child of the universe, back to where you began
Where we belong   all one
Solitary   silent   sentient

memorials de Mountainair, Highway 60, New Mexico

Passage of Years

after a certain amount of time, logical, reasonable
passage of years
different for everyone, there isn't a conscious sense
of death anymore, the loss
doesn't physically hurt, more like rubbing
against a scar,
aware of the wound, memory telling the soul
what to feel. Ever present, my existence
apparently regardless
of the passage of years, a dozen years,
no longer black or dark,
gray, yes,
cloudy still, chilled
shades of imagination
not of regrets but rather
what might have been

Quantified Love

I loved you fiercely
unreservedly
till the end
of your days

one kiss a day,
eleven thousand three hundred fifteen
at my reckoning
and I know
it's at least double

I loved you more
than one kiss a day...
infinitely more.

Advice

soul's ghost of laughter hangs
in melancholy blanket of memory
recessed,
coaxed out through moments of forgetfulness

cobwebs dance on soundless chord
echoing driftless through
wearisome weight, lethargic mist

a method of madness
tempering this human being
with flexible frailty
survival cloaked in sadness,
sanity's burden of proof

I heard this recently—if you fall, protect your head
gray matter
at all costs.
A blow to the noggin' can kill you.
Good advice

once in a lifetime…

When I First Loved You

when I first loved you
that year, 1969, innocence
we discovered commonalities
on all night drives, lost in the city
ending up in Stillwater, across the Mississippi
to watch the sunrise

a natural, easy progression
when I first loved you
weaving a foundation
we built upon
a footing
to spring from

summer, June, groovin' on acid
and Neil Young's "Cowgirl in the Sand"
when I first loved you
Cupid's arrow surprising,
piercing
to fuse the imperceptible
continuous circle
then the Hollywood moment—
tractor beam
eyes riveted,
when I first loved you
locked in
quickening stare, cheeks crimson

epiphany

rising
from dilapidated, horsehair chairs
floating breathlessly
across space, arms twining tender embrace
when I first loved you
pulling

closer and closer
into eternity

hearing only
the tandem beating
ba bump, ba bump, ba bump,
one heart-melding mind, spirit, love

without end

Moonglow

e'en's birth

banishes coral sun

orb's hypnotic brilliance

beckons, "come away, let go...."

Mesmerize   entrance this soul

with violet hued mountain shadows

rising   at my fingertips

brush strokes

painting

the Gila

Does Time Heal All?

Don't push; be respectful
of my wishes, especially
my grief.
Don't bulldoze me,
running over
my convictions, my positions.
Don't frustrate
what meager control I cling to.
Empower me;
encourage me
to take charge of my life, owning
my feelings, expressing them
firmly, unequivocally, arguing
my will,
my intent,
my belief.
Support me
when you don't agree and
if that's not possible
then step aside
while I claw
my way back.
No apologies.
Spurning overtures
directed my way, I absolutely
avoid
any milieu
of that sort,
being too volatile,
vulnerable,
raw.
I am better
but so limited, so defined
by boundaries
too narrow,
too constricting

by the growing reality
of his absence.
It is true—
this did happen
to me,
a widow whose married life
disintegrated,
in those few jolting seconds.

And then today
feeling better—honestly—
tears not all dried up,
not even very far away,
but owning a sense of
accomplishment, cautiously
upbeat, being tempered by experience, not knowing what
will be, what
tomorrow will bring…
who's guaranteed tomorrow?
The life force demands
preparation
to remain,
preparation
to succeed and bear
the valley of the shadow,
dealing with
tomorrows
as if we have innumerable,
acutely aware
the vulnerability
of what we are.
Resisting medication

not wanting an alteration

to whom I am—

I've lost too much,

wanting
to hold onto
truth and purity of feelings,
my emotions—
ME.
After ten and a half months,
I'm beginning
to get used to it,
this life. Time is
my friend,
helper,
salvation… till
the moment passes.

contemplative hope-filled gaze

My Life

Cerro Pedernal, the infamous northern New Mexico landmark…
the mesa peak I always wanted to hike up
but in the years I lived so near, just a few miles away
past Youngsville between Coyote and Gallina,
I never attempted it   and now?
The peak requires a steep hike on very loose rock,
a short, Class 3 wall,
and a narrow, exposed trail eight miles up and back.
I just may have missed this one
now bowing to my muscles that require continual preservation
or maybe it's conservation, nonetheless, definite limits
undeniable but am not ready to admit defeat.
Certainly limits that can be quite unforgiving
at this stage of my life,
for instance, I'm resigned to no more cartwheels.
Well, pretty much.
I'm forced to be reasonable, sensible, oof,
I do not like that moniker
but now I often have conversations with my peers
about mindfulness
exhorting them   and me   to watch where we walk
to avoid missteps, to stay upright.
DON'T FALL! especially when I consider the consequences,
how traumatic brain injury may be the result.
They say aging is not for sissies. It's a shock, that gut check
noticing the changes now so blatantly undisguised
Drooping lids, jowls, neck waddle following down, down, down
to these appaloosa legs, one might say roan.
Mottled, spotted, splotchy,
red and purply stippled. I wonder if I could be reshod.
Arms peppered, freckled brown spots like a connect the dots puzzle.
The gray streaked mane, tow head to platinum, even though gradual
it was notable the year that it happened.
Did you know that green chili synthesizes collagen,
reduces inflammation for healthier aging?
Now that's the best reason for consuming

vast amounts of my favorite stew.
I'm truly not that obsessed with the decade's effects
upon this body,
it simply continues to make me notice and appreciate the days,
the years that are waning as they take their toll,
unescapable father time.
I evaluate what's treasured, and of course, family is paramount.
Precious photos in my faded albums, innocent,
tender smiling faces,
the imprints etched deeply within my heart.
Those old albums are stored
with easy access, staged for rescue from any disaster.
Possessions are one thing, I'd relinquish them all,
save for those memories
stored in 3 x 3 images. I take some comfort in the fact that
I live in the middle,
New Mexico, far from rising oceans,
oceans that possess too much melancholy for me personally.
I don't mind being ruined for a beachfront dwelling.
I ponder all of the ones that have passed on,
try to make sense of loss and I must resign questions to fate,
a conscious effort to let go and release those to the other side
submitting to the seasons as trees shed their leaves
transmogrifying back to the earth.
What's happened to my face, my body,
tells the story of experience,
the love, the laughter, the tears
I speak gratefulness to the lumps and lines,
the hues and patterns that weave history and memory together
in one unique crazy quilt
blanketing my shoulders, wrapping it around and around
absolving absorbing the imprint every single thread holds
the richly designed material of life
 as gentle waves resonate within my spirit,
understanding is my song.

Sacred Remnants

it only took five years
to relinquish the splintered heart
cobbled together,

soldered into jagged lightning strike lines
to close the abyss—
buried dreams fade into shadows

veiled in undulating
electrostatic storm of brain waves unable
to connect understanding with experience

you graze the edge of my soul
with hammering silence, I keep my distance,
I'm adrift,

swirling in waves, thrashing to surmount the riptide,
as I sling my feet over the edge of the bed
willing myself awake

emerge the cocoon of slumbering respite
sunrise calls   spirit to spirit
orange sphere inching

eyes squinting in unison
against stark rays of blinding reality
to traverse the mountainous hurdle

now six years, then seven
and twenty years later the mended heart
is no longer where I left it

On Tenterhooks

I am afraid to love you as much as I could   determining the
cosseted course   where I can continue to breathe   armor
intact   I know what it feels like to lose   promising all your
days to bargain for one more with the lost   Murder   slaugh-
tering the simplest thought   short-circuiting synapses driving
insane   rampaging bull through the soul   ripping the heart
into foreign fragments   the most exquisite pain   searing
burrowing into loathsome rivulets of sulfurous need the day life
ceased   with no choice or voice in destiny   hating that verdict
that inimitable crux where light goes black   breath exudes   a
finality that is forever   forever   forever

Defensible Space

Isolation is one sentinel against heartbreak, to live in a vacuum
the ghost of laughter hanging like gossamer memory's
burdensome yoke,
grafted like an inscription,
embedded tattoo branded by fate.
Can we heal ourselves? We hope
expecting
to meet such audacious endeavor with open spirit
anticipating relief even a single deep breath can bring
in that abode where no ear perceives or eye dare glimpse
the jagged wound etched into the marrow
and sinew of a shattered psyche.
Impenetrable, unintelligible from the visible character,
it is coaxed out
by moments of forgetfulness whereupon learned performance,
cloaking sadness with a tentative mantle, may extinguish the flame
may even pass for [ostensibly] health, portraying well-being
while in truth an umbrella of disillusionment,
the fog of human frailty
and vulnerability, allowing no access to psychosis,
persists with suffocating weight.
In high fire areas of the desert and mountains,
residents are encouraged to clear a perimeter of thirty feet,
to cut all brush and incendiary materials for security.
I imagine my arms outstretched thirty feet thwarting access
to my soul, my 'dwelling' that remains private, circumspect.
My defensible space.

A Singular Drive... 285

Born and bred in the Midwest
my spirit's forever yearned for the mountains
where eons past roots pierced canyon walls taking shape across
this cholla gardened desert-scape
sage brush, piñon, scrub oaks, ponderosa pine
foothills ascending to rocky climes softly hued
along coral clay   then   gradually blending
with hunter green, grayish blue caste in distant outline
I tune my ears, hearing secrets, only my soul comprehends
nature's tacit voices that softly suss with whispers
as swaying branches nudge tumbleweeds
along fence lines to congregate, commiserate in arroyos
celestial covering frosts peaks
defining the separation with haze shrouded mounds
earthly to ethereal but I view it as one
in this treasured tierra, my center, an anchor
with cords reaching beyond the expanse
I'm suspended between, a transplanted Gemini
from cloudy tundra to glorious sun filled sky
idyllic blessing I revere   drinking in my remarkable time
to drive heavenward   285   the road winding,
chest rising, inhaling oxygen along with awe
I am imbued
with enchantment.

Cross My Heart

New Mexico has a heartbreaking practice of consecrating their inordinate amount of traffic deaths depicted in the following poem:

Across this state
I'm counting crosses
12, 13, stories buried, 14, 15,
memorializing someone's life and death
to help us remember, ponder, relate to the loss, 16,
"my son is late," mother says, "dinner will wait,"
17, 18, 19, 20, too, too many gathered
with plastic piles and white Styrofoam bits,
pop bottles, beer cans, cardboard boxes at rest where you
died
21, "it can't be," she murmurs to the uniformed harbinger
at the door, uttered phrase, "we regret to inform"
collapsed in shock, can hear no other sound
22, 23, 24, and 3 more makes 27 if there's a heaven, I hope
they're there
What if I stopped to say a prayer?
28, 29, 30, now a green fender, car case, billowing
WalMart sack clings to cat claw
over dilapidated sofa, an orange pail, would it help
if I paid tribute?
31, 32, you were loved by someone, maybe many
a daughter, grandson, spouse, best friend
now making a fresh make-shift grave
highway workers respect what we'll never forget,
spangled, glittery, gloriously gaudy
33, 34 trying to reflect the light they were in our eyes—
theirs forever shuttered with black.
5 in a row was the worst I observed.
Carnage.
Autocide.
Curly shredded tire cords
carrying semis laded with our necessities,
maybe that blow-out planted a cross,

shattered the thread of life,
inscribed, all caps [M-I-S-S-I-N-G] under a flag
of blue jeans draped on spindling shrub.
35, 36 two spirits woven as one; a young woman's
smiling face
could not escape   the appointment.
71 on this route today...
I'm counting crosses
across this state.

Serenity

peaceful spirit
give me leave to fly
beyond temporal
amid   lofty horizons

blessed Bahia Samara, Costa Rica

Fix

you want to make it all right
you want to fix everything
with the flick of a switch
the wave of a wand
it will work out
that's what your heart says
that's what your intention hears
that you can do it
you won't accept any less
it is how the nurturing heart is wired
that the underdog
that the hungry and lonely
the needy and lost
can be fixed
so simple
and yet never easy
I will say the thing
the right thing, do something
that makes a difference
that brings a smile
confidence and inspiration
remedy along with
answers…
if only

Talk to Me-- As soon as they come out of you, they're leaving

Ungrateful little shits, twits
you made us learn computers,
our brains on overload,
we just wanted to talk to you
but noooo,
you'd only email but soon after we mastered that—
oh, now it's fucking facebook,
you cannot be bothered with email,
and do instagram
if you ever want another picture
but I resist, rebel
on the grounds that your voice is what I crave, ears hungering
for kind words that show you care
enough to actually call, converse
on the other end of this damned device. Is it too much to ask,
a heart to heart, after squeezing you out
of my lady parts?!

Christmas Lost

Soon,
they'll all arrive,
to pervade empty spaces,

permeate and
disguise silence
to bring

energy,
a vestige of living,
someone

to come home to, something
to tranquilize
ringing ears.

Dry, starved, needy,
lonely, forlorn, depressed
I hate this person

entrapped underneath
the onerous blanket
of grief.

"Pay no heed to that man behind… "
ashamed, I won't let them see
the steady vibration inside

pulsating loss,
of mendacious shadows
in the nadir where I reside,

the continuum   survival.
A sort of auto pilot,
compelling me

to strive until   exhausted
I kiss them and wave
goodbye.

Hey, what doesn't kill you… (to be or not to be)

There's always something to be sad about
if that's what we choose
    [to be]

A child starving or abused
the lonely soul in the old folks home

children so far away – grandchildren farther
with no time to care, to share a note, a call

the soldier's lost limbs or mind
or shipped home in a box

the homeless, too poor to matter
too poor to escape

a single mom selling her body
to pay rent, feed kids

suicide inveigling your dearest friend
after she promised she'd stay

you beg, in vain, as the light in love's eye
is doused (dying in your arms)

the son that gets cancer then divorced
A thick scar running the length of a heart—

it survived and now doubtless is the toughest part
and strongest element of the wizened soul

there's always something to be sad about
or we may choose
    [not to be]

Who Let Go?

Harried cacophony, busy shoppers hastening along
crowded sidewalk
the press disorienting, I could only see thigh high;
over-coats, pantlegs, parcels, purses nudging me
I was holding your hand and looked up and you were not Papa
I must have let go, then took the next hand without looking up
but it wasn't Papa's
a stranger looked down to see whose tiny hand he had clenched
and in that second of perception
everything ceased. Movement, sound, breath, security
Life.   My life.   Fear paralyzing every cell
Didn't Papa notice I'd let go?
It was maybe a minute in all, not even enough time for tears
before the familiar gray fedora, the plaid muffler appeared
ten feet ahead
searching, piercing through the crowd to retrieve
his stunned five year old.
Reaching me he clasped my hand,
obliviously continuing to Murphy's hardware.
He discovered the same little girl he had lost
but I bore an imprint,
changed indelibly, distilled in character;
anxiety   panic   loss
tattooed
Papa never knew
Did I let go, or did you?

Glorious Rain

And then the rains came.
The air smells full, fresh, dispersing smoky atmosphere
I inhale deeply filling lungs with moisture laden oxygen

renewing blood cells, clearing brain waves,
 the drops begin, one at a time, almost inaudibly
nonetheless real, I strain to hear,
petitioning the heavens to open

to release life giving offering into nature's extended arms.
She heeds my prayer sending a benediction,
now a symphony pummeling the west portal
no longer intermittent…

a deluge streaming down gutters, flushing leaves,
twigs, pine needles
into low lying puddles, gushing to ditches
OH   OH   but then
diminishing,   OH,   not yet,
and my supplication does not alter the universe

instead, my hopeful heart scans the skyline
for that glorious arc, miracle of the gods,   radiant colors
I feel it before I see it, sensing the pressure,

then   the singular hue of gray, green, yellowish cast
where sun, clouds, and moist air merge in dazzling array,
simply, effortlessly, a tour de force

every time, without fail,
delighted and enthralled as if it were my first,
a rainbow virgin,

Standing, transfixed
thanking the powers that be for this blessing
after the rains came.

spellbinding Burro Mountain alchemy

Sojourner

I will stay and be present until I escape
this disparate life
with pristine facade masking
ugly underbelly, cold and gloom
quite impossible year 'round.
Quite.

Undercurrent laced conversations
promote jealousy, competition
in small town America.

Long winter month's coop
invariably leads to a shift,
a rotation of sorts necessary
to quell hen-house pecking. Pulling back
from one, aligning with another,
delicately side-stepping

or indelicately,
the infraction,
the slight,
imagined or real, as winter closes in
so does withdrawal.
Cherishing longtime friends, I anticipate
leaving them.

Wrapped in down comforter, both arms
woven, cocooning security
sheathing body and mind, spirit
from December's certain siege.
The begrudging smile,
"you're the lucky one,"   (undertow, Bitch)
packing up, driving alone the 1700 miles
one, two, three days
to an alternate universe.

Doting Nana morphs into
writer, partner, mountain denizen.

It's a magnet, familiar itching,
the challenge to stretch
out of my comfort zone
to be energized
by fresh alliances, unique influence
pouring in
to the stratum of experience,

which seems to have become as essential as breath
but not only—it is health to the psyche, sanity—
though at times I could say it, in itself, makes me crazy or
maybe just a bit unhinged.

Infectious wanderlust,
undeniable dreams,
the impetus to encounter each day
as sojourner.

So Lost

An eerily penetrating howl ricochets
through the cavern echoing from ponderosa to cactus
hurling its vibration across the arroyo

to settle like fine dust
upon the fresh kill
with eyes closed I strain to listen more acutely

as a slight tremor shudders from the base of my spine
tingling to the top of my head, I have to discern, decide,
is it better to lie still, run, or slither

in what I divine is the opposite direction
wisdom eludes me having lain so long
amid desert dark horizon,
disorienting my typical acuity, the damning message
emitted from god knows where
after long minutes, another clue
the pack of yipping coyotes, I guess,
a hundred yards down the canyon
lone stars at random peek through clouds

no more illuminating
than that first howl... it's not the first time
I've lost my way.

soothing sands de Playa Rosada, Costa Rica

Always Reaching

longing moves the soul to belong
to a tribe
shifting with sands of time
to find safety, innately attuned to sanctuary
where a gentle shoreline
changes quite imperceptibly with seasons

decades where generations
couldn't even imagine, let alone realize
lofty dreams,
no
the staid and stolid stalwarts
faded under glaring scrutiny
like sun drenched furniture
scrubbed, sanded and stained
once useful, now aged beyond synergy
into obscurity, finally
discarded, buried brittle bones,
not unlike
those aspirations of
past goals
begging the question,
is it too late?

Angst

The angst these days so familiar
 so prescient, I'm adopting it as my natural state
along with exhaustion, frustration and melancholy
because as much as I endeavor to assuage it,
the futility grinds and pulverizes my peace.
Peace
It fades in and out, a florid scene
like the TV screen breaking into grainy pixels
I make an imperceptible adjustment
the picture forms   finally
that I might interpret, limitless effort seizing
what I long to understand
Understand
as heart melds with soul,
spirit divining my mind's eye
to grasp wonders reflected in gentle waves
of kindness and grace
Grace
draped with patience
giving light and depth to hard questions
choosing
to balance good and evil,
one welcome, one necessary

Me Too Mother
(written before the 2018 midterm elections)

THE ONLY MOTHER YOU WILL EVER HAVE
I am a petulant child's paragon of patience,
indulging my spoiled brat, slightly afraid of my rebellious teen,
I have given humanity, oh say, four billion years to 'find' yourself.
Nurturing Gaia, primal mother, vilified victim of abuse
WHAT ABOUT ME?
You think you have been assaulted?!
Raping my forests, you denuded the majestic Redwoods.
Ninety-five percent destroyed. Hacked down,
gorging greedy desire.
Who tried to save Minnesota's forests in 1902? HA! Women.
Maria Sanford and Florence Bramhall
establishing the Chippewa National Forest.
Fertility goddess, Demeter, deified harvester
battling forces eradicating vital species, holding treasures
in delicate balance while artifacts dissolve to dust
Now   envision the subjugating practice of shearing women
expiating men's frustration over defeat in battle,
making women the scapegoat with punishing brutality.
You argue God insists on the mandatory shaved head?
"God requires," the religious fanatic's justification.
Men controlling my body.
Olympian Goddess of wisdom, Athena, most courageous
and resourceful, intervene, armor us to do battle
"I was pushed from behind into a bedroom, pushed onto the
bed and Brett got on top of me. His hands pinned me down,
then a hand over my mouth to stop me from screaming.
I thought that Brett was accidentally going to kill me."
Choking off oxygen, my bountiful landscape is parched,
polluted, tortured with lethal gasses, herbicides, pesticides,
chemicals heaped with CFCs reaching the stratosphere,
ultraviolet radiation,
chlorine atoms erasing the critical ozone layer.
Who will address poisoned drinking water,
ensuring the Great Lakes are not reduced to

dumping grounds for industry? Habitat for fish ruined as the
oil-slick Cuyahoga River flowed like burning lava in '69.
Finally convinced, lawmakers passed the Clean Water Act
inspiring the 1st Earth Day in 1970.
Fortyfifth's administration's roll back of EPA rules
on a crash course to unequivocally decimate our water systems.
Thetis, hang on. Keep struggling to survive;
your life-giving water runs with our tears.
The Kansas Corporation Commission has had to further restrict
the amount of oilfield wastewater injected underground
in the hopes of reducing the staggering number of
earthquakes in the region. It's too toxic to dump above ground;
injections upsetting the balance
between layers of rock deep underground,
causing that rock to shift and generate tremors.
EARTHQUAKES!
Persephone's gut roils, contracts.
Dilated, groaning to expel a stillborn entity.
"I was too afraid and ashamed to tell anyone the details.
I tried to convince myself that because Brett did not rape me,
I should be able to move on and just pretend that
it had never happened."
Vak Devi, flood us with truth, with the power of words that express
and expose, that cannot be silenced,
radiance piercing the shadows.
Are we complicit? What can I do?

VOTE

Elect responsible and environmentally strident people to our
governing bodies.

ME TOO!

YOU TOO!

ALL OF US!

Dawn into Dusk

Suzan Dawn   9/30/48-1/22/09

     All I can say now is—
I miss you dear friend
         I wonder
      about all the unanswered
unanswerable questions
    knowing
your pain was unbearable, your loss
beyond
what your heart could endure.

I knew and was aware
      it hurt that much,
I knew
        the taut thread to sanity....
     SNAP!
    whirling,
    swirling irretrievably
    into murky shadow, enticed with the web of delusion
        and infinite sleep
          of amnesty,
It's so hard for us
control freaks to be
out of control
weak
vulnerable
confused
We don't choose to live there
but
when circumstances dictate,
            then the soul
              the spirit
              the heart
          must find peace
           and let go....
Even the herculean effort to

fill your asthmatic lungs with enough air
              barely enough,
            never to capacity,
            grew beyond your ability.
It ceased.
    At the last
   breath flowing away
from you
        unconstrained
       beneath the shroud.
I am free now
        in your truth
       as I hear the unutterable.
No more afraid of my perceived complicity—
    not responsible
    but all one,
    in the human family.
It wasn't as much me you left
but him you went to.
    Let it go.
I relinquish my dissension, [at least in this one circumstance]
    always striving for the underdog, chasing
      a happy ending to right the injustice.

    IT'S NOT FUCKING FAIR!
I will never accept the status quo;
    "speaking words of wisdom, let it be"
      Let it be?
  My lifelong search for the illusive balance continues;
    to obtain, to apprehend….water through my fingers.
   Maybe they're right.
   Goddamn Beatles.

forever Mesa Poleo friends, Mady and Suzan

What Matters?

Why don't we matter to each other?
I have my own agenda. It's my life.
I'm selfish, self-absorbed, self-pitying.
Leave me alone, everyone, but I need you.

Do we matter to each other? Enough
to give the homeless a meal in a dead friend's name?
"This is from Suzan."
I don't explain she died seven years ago.
She mattered.

They look at me with grateful eyes
robbed of hope, devoid of care.
Who do they matter to?
I don't give cash because I want them to have food
not a bottle. You be the judge. That's what I do.
It's not pejorative, I'm a mom. They need food,
even if it is fast food.

I'm surprised I don't haul along a bag of fruits and vegetables
whenever I leave the house,
but they'd make my vehicle smell
and attract flies.
Is that what matters?!

Yeah, but it's a new car.

Delight Song (My True Self)
          inspired by N. Scott Momaday

I am memories that float and fade, billowy clouds
pale to opaque
I am wilted crepe paper poppy petals
spent with thirst
I am icicles hanging from my heart
impenetrably locked
I am desert rose marble
split by lightning
I am a willow bent to the earth
weeping for shelter
I am a sticky spider web of doubts
straining for release

You see, I am alive, I am alive

I stand in good relation to adversity
Vak Devi
I stand in good relation to teacher
Athena
I stand in good relation to understanding
Gaia
I stand, a honed blade tempered by experience

You see, I am alive, and I have flourished through all of this.

imagination lies beyond the horizon

Mother Nature, Killer Beeaach

Arizona Sun Times headline:
Real Estate Values Soar as West Coast Sinks Into Ocean
(Retirees in Arizona and Nevada surfing off
their new beachfront property)

We leave her scant choice (Our Mother), she has to fight back
unleashing furious, ferocious floods with a monster el Niño
"You've done it now, I am pissed," she thunders,
"taste the tempestuous super typhoons
toppling entire towns or
how 'bout a micro burst hurling airplanes to earth
like a falcon stoop
or some devastating drought fanning fatal firenados?"

Each storm coins new and exciting terms,
breaking previous records
as aroused meteorologist
exudes warnings like a steroid stuffed ball player.
Lightning, tsunami, oh my! Earthquake, volcano, oh my!!
Polar vortex, bombogenesis, oh my!!!
Mercy Mother.

And what is our response?
Keep spewing carbons, raping strata,
depleting reserves that delicately balance eco systems,
destroy habitat, annihilate species, trees, insects, monarchs…
oh, we're an evolved planet, alright!
"Not much longer," Mother warns.

Dear Diary

I do not want to be
a part
of your life,
I want to
BE
your life.
That's a sick, narcissistic thought
I immediately realized;
he'd be possessed
I'd be smothered, devoured,
FLEEING
for the nearest exit.
Disney ruined me
with Prince Charming.
AS IF!!
I don't even want to be
a princess,
pink is really
not my color,
and glass slippers? They'd surely
KILL
my bunions.

AKA Yeti

When I told my son-in-law, Mikhal,
"he has a size 13 shoe,"
he quipped, "Ahhhh, that's why you like him."
He's Russian, Mikhal, doesn't mince words,
maybe it's cultural

I didn't know about Harley guys, that's the 13er
Harley Fuckin' Davidson,
she's a jealous bitch!
How you deck all out for her
leather cap, shades, and sleek chaps
an orange and black bandanna
embracing your neck,
you rev, she responds
How do I compete
with that?

It did not take too long to see
she wouldn't suffer me,
couldn't get comfortable, blown to bits,
teeth jarring ride, trying to hide
my chagrin, savoring the thrill
'a good sport' until
we dumped

You forgot to tell me
"keep your feet on the pegs," so I pinned my leg
as her weight cackled I Am Conqueror,
CRACK! CRACK!
Hearing the snap,
two breaks ended that wretched affair
with the Harley Fuckin' Davidson,   but not him

Now he rides solo
What will I do? I'm
stickin' with
his size thirteen shoe

I Have No Defense

What the hell was I thinking?
Me?!
What were you thinking?
There's no excuse, quibbling,
justifying such an outburst
as if
as if I'm a beach ball getting tossed
and dropped
lobbed across the expanse
like yesterday's rubbish
What the hell was I thinking
letting you
convince me
again
with those
inane regrets?

Ersatz Liaison (Unplugged)

we made an appointment…
no media allowed
two's company, iPhone's a crowd
we looked into present eyes
that did not hedge or try to lie
clearly connected
sincerely interested
fully aware and
forgive me if I stare
but I'm incredulous
though pleasantly surprised
two years together and I didn't know
you have blue eyes!

reality   or   perception of power

Arenal Volcano, Alajuela Province, Costa Rica

Remember Loneliness

How can I be responsible for your insecurities?
Will you be for mine?
             I have to fix myself
Scales drop from my eyes.
    You snapped
                  with such unwarranted venom,
I took the outburst extremely ill, we tried
without success
                  to mend, apologize,
placate
and put it in its proper perspective but
too little reflection

too much togetherness, not enough
understanding... I could only sleep
with Xanax.

Then the silent ride
                  to Albuquerque from Santa Fe
balloon fiesta (woohoo!)

hardening the arteries
                  of acumen until
                  finally back home

pushing the elephant into the center of the room,
"You talked down to me, made me feel inferior,"
astonished by his accusation
aghast, I insisted,
"You couldn't be more wrong.
I think you're smart, talented, sensitive
             [stroke, stroke, stroke]

you misperceived my comments,"
reiterating, as if he didn't know,
my sassiness, brassiness, and in your face

honesty—will he bail?
Do I compromise,
do I walk on eggshells? First exhibition
of temper, moodiness.
    Manageable, shocking?

Suck it up, I think,
                for now. How much do I
    have to adapt, balance,

for him to be alright with me?

How many layers of questions, revelations?
Good to figure this shit out before I sell my house.

Circle of Belonging

ripples of water   moisture laden circles
diversity exemplified
all marvelously extending from and through one another
youth   aged   diminutive   ample,   I feel the energy
generated fluently perpetuating placid fluctuation
balanced dance, swirling life continuum in and of itself
dichotomy of encapsulated liberty   to alter perception
awareness reaching outward   offering,
transcending singularity with inclusive overtures
radiating images from black to white
obscure to pure   from center,
the middle effecting each sphere
able to accomplish as a conglomerate
what the individual requires all unique, not one identical
and   yet unity portrays such simplicity of purpose
for those of us that choose to see it
overlapping, the invisible bond
holding each other
in that place of belonging.

Fly, My Lovelies

I barely dared to look over the edge. It was safe, snuggly nestled, sheltered in place. After a year in isolation I was cautiously optimistic. First vaccination down, one to go, two weeks more to be fully vaccinated and then what?

There's the question. What is prudent? I was an endangered species stuck in isolation for all of a year unable to travel, fly, visit my family and friends, prohibited from society. Sinking into depression surrounded by my morose attitude I fed my spirit with books and media. It did not work. I tried to fortify myself, attempting to persuade my psyche that it could always be worse. I could have the virus, I could die, I must be grateful, patient.

Month after month the numbers rose, the horror stories increased, and I prayed for my loved ones and for those families suffering incredible pain and overwhelming loss. Rising up just enough to peer over I peeked out from the top of my bubble and saw too many acting business as usual, much to my chagrin. Chanting we are free, we deny your scare tactics, I ducked back down under my barricade. And this heartbreaking statement from a naysayer, "Why should I care about others?!" Cold-hearted, not afraid to voice such a preposterous sentiment. I cannot let it impact me, allow my integrity to be tainted by such bile. It is too easy to be influenced, sucked into negativity, anger and hate. I will not do it.

That is my prayer. My goal. To be the gentle contener, spreading grace, blanketing positive energy over and out to the universe.

My wings are unfurled and fluffed, as I hop up onto the perimeter, flexing my legs, I get ready to spring, to catch the gentle breeze that will lift me out of the doldrums, no longer stuck, ridding myself of fear, shedding those loose feathers weighing me down. I fill my lungs, one, two, three times, fledging into the unknown.

Perennial Life

"Just beyond the flower garden at the end of the lawn
the curvature of the earth begins ... "

I lost sight of the future enmeshed in old growth
buried under fallow ground,
driving the spade beneath crusted shell there is life below
where stunted thoughts, dreams and visions reside.
I knew if I separated them, gave them a glimpse
of what they could become, there was still a chance…
you simply needed someone's notice, mine,
some tending or cultivation. Dormant how many years,
neglected but not forgotten, a wellspring of bounty
if you can but try. Do not despair, let hope sprout,
bursting forth,
reaching for light, oxygen, nourishment
till your garden bears fruit again.
I kept heading out to the yard, in search of myself,
looking for the solace and sanctuary I'd known.
Nurturing the landscape all of my years
it took some months to decide
if I even wanted to dig into the neglected morass.
An old pond,
the arid shell all that remained, could not serve.
A ten inch layer of pine needles burying what treasure?
I do relish a welcoming outdoor space
and a challenge. Digging in, ripping away,
laying bare parched earth,
it seemed every day I delighted in treasures. An iron bell,
soothing gong, deep, subtle, then pottery shards,
some with paint still visible.
I did bring my favorites from Iowa
when I relocated to the Southwest; more iron ornaments,

bamboo wind chime, the brain coral smuggled
from Mexico and a plethora of rocks.
Who transports pounds and pounds of rocks
across the United States? Me. As well as those
hauled from partner's ranch in the Burros.
Day after day, while my back held up,
I fashioned the overgrowth into a welcoming
peaceful place I could invite you into, rearranging
the trash barrels so they were not a focal point,
moving them out of the walled yard where they'd sat
atop a two by four foot piece of drywall.
Picking it up I was astounded to discover
the underside was a glass mosaic with floral motif.
The background, white squares, in varied sizes,
almost half of them fallen off, but the most superb
were vivid purple and lavender delphinium
with 3D petals, ribbed with curling edges.
I sat down on the ground marveling
at how someone could have abandoned it.
(more story material, hah, now imagining various
scenarios; it was a gift from an old lover, or possibly,
some wretched reminder better left under the garbage.)
Ecstatic, I was divining how I would retrieve the fallen
pieces, bring it back to life.
Several days later I decided on the fix.
Determining if I couldn't replicate the original,
I would paint a sunset on the upper portion
putting my own signature on it. Coral, shades of yellow,
and silvery blue filled in an evening sky,
the backdrop adorning my yard. Placed against the wall,
just beyond the flower garden at the end of the lawn,
I step through the portal, beyond the sunset,
breaking free, where the curvature of the earth begins.

Itsy Bitsy Spider

I look up from my bed just before lights out
and see a spider at the edge of the ceiling.

Will he torture me with a disturbing noise,
the one that says I'm going to crawl into your ear…
like an earworm, a song that embeds itself into my psyche,
sticky music, stuck song syndrome,
not to be confused with auditory hallucinations
technically known as palinacousis!
Look it up.

Holy shit!
No wonder I can't sleep or if I get to sleep, can't stay asleep,
waking at 2—   turning to see 3, then 3:34
at which time I pick up my pen
and write down all the thoughts plaguing me,
brilliant ideas that I'm afraid I won't recall in the morning,
like this tripe. Good Lord, rather a waste of time, eh?
I believe it will help me purge angst, allowing slumber

Where was I?
Looking at the spider.
I've read until my eyes crossed
but as soon as I closed the book
my spider took over with the song.
Itsy bitsy spider climbed down the wall, up my nose
and now walks around behind my left eye.
Is that why my vision is blurred?
If I asked my ophthalmologist about that,
what do you suppose he'd say?
He diagnosed a retinal nevus.
Look it up.

The spider was gone this morning.
Where do you think it is?

Pragmatist

Interminable maneuvering in order
to get a good night's sleep;
ear plugs, medication, an occasional puff, puff,
then separate bedrooms, now coined "sleep divorce"
It really didn't occur to me
I'd miss him
so little.
Now that he's gone I sleep
with my pen.

I Thought This Would Last Forever

after so much resistance I tried you-
you wore me down
friends exhorted me to give it a shot
"you don't know what you're missing
involvement, new experiences, different perspective
all good, no downside, it's time to put yourself out there"
so I tiptoed in, cautiously, maintaining skepticism
wanting control, independence,
my walled space—
testing the waters, ankle deep, waist deep
oh, this isn't so complicated, not so scary
I just might be able to do this
and then you changed,
OVERNIGHT,
upgrades unfamiliar to me, my comfort zone challenged
not recognizing the person I'd morphed into,
I did try, for several months to be you
but I have to go back
to my peaceful place
fall from grace
can't keep pace
I had no faith…
a trolling virgin erased
even though
you genuinely didn't care about me, and now
I'm an anti-social-media-meme

Is All Love Schizo?

disillusioned coward slinking away
missing the potential treasure, bowing to fear
relationship foretells,
burrowing its peril into the soul, avoiding risk

one defense is mediocrity settling into
good enough … harnessed feelings
heart's barricade
in an effort to dodge injury
the savored memory
an impression of fingertips on skin, slightly tangible
into your shoulder blades when I wrapped round,
breastpress against chest

spirit threads through energy
reminiscent of love's depth
how could I know
it was our final kiss

longing takes hold, heart groans
rising with sweet love's meld, soul's tryst
with savored finish, sensual ardor
in sated surrender

 the maze of imagination comforts even as it tortures
moth to flame   extinguished
in a puff of smoke
I flew too close

A Life in Process

Still so much fragility in me,
hidden by bravado.

The tears pour over a welling
of my lower lid
to cheeks
that anticipate anointing.

I lick my lip and it's salty,
and I miss the taste of my sweet love.

Sitting on this faded plum, nylon chair
you bought,
I don't remember where or when,
but you scoured the back roads along the Mississippi
before you discovered it,
paying twenty dollars.

Better than that was the wrong turn onto gravel,
"I found this clearing enclosed by walnuts and red oak,"
you'd tell me, knowing I'd fix a picnic basket
and we'd spend a sun-bathed fall afternoon there
immersed
in the nature
of each other.

I can still close my eyes
and feel your soft breath
in my ear
six years after the ocean
called your name.

Acknowledgements

With gratitude to the magazines in which these poems first appeared.

- Puzzle Zen
- Moonglow
- A Singular Drive
- A Life in Process   **Writing In A Woman's Voice**

- Hey, What Doesn't Kill You
- It's None Of Your Fucking Business

                       Tuck Magazine

- Hey, What Doesn't Kill You
- Advice
- A Life in Process
- Cross My Heart
- Passage of Years
- So Lost   **Poetic Bond VII, VIII, IX, X**

- A Life in Process
- Land of my Heart   **Lyrical Iowa**

- Quantified Love   **Human to Human**

Hippie at Heart

What I Used To Be, I Still Am

Lynne Zotalis

Hippie at Heart Review:
https://www.amazon.com/dp/B08DC6GZ7T

"Hippie At Heart: What I Used to Be, I Still Am is a shockingly tender, truthful, tragic tale of resiliency and hope. Ms. Zotalis writes with immediacy and clarity. I found myself immersed in the memoir from the first page to the very end and had difficulty putting the book down to get on with what needed to be done in my day. Zotalis' accounts of her survival in a home where demonstrative love was in short supply, the ultimate betrayal by someone she adored, her rebelion, drug use and the ultimate back-to-nature sojourn in Northern New Mexico, the pendulum effect of a cult-like Christian evangelical experience, and finding a centered grounded life with the love of her life and her children made fascinating reading. All of this framed by a tragedy that may have never been overcome but, instead, integrated into a life fully lived."

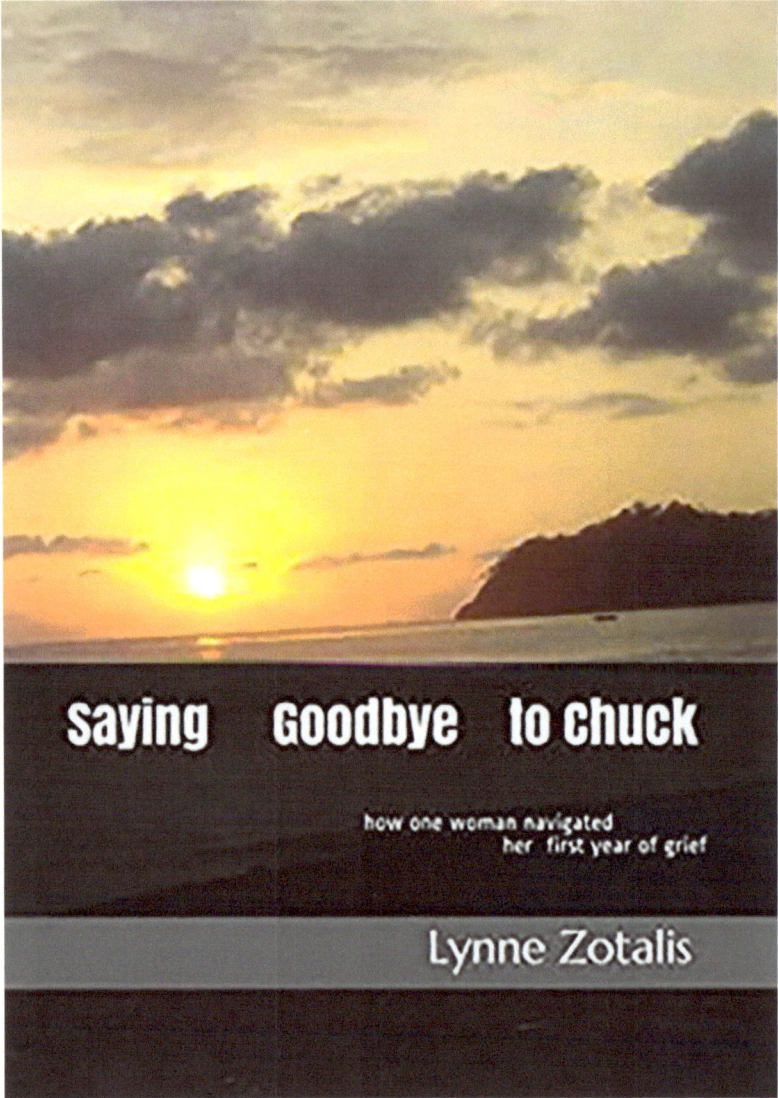

saying   Goodbye   to chuck

how one woman navigated
her first year of grief

Lynne Zotalis

Saying Goodbye to Chuck inspires and encourages victims of loss to be in the moment with their grief. So distressed by books that pushed me into wholeness and resolve by the end of the manuscript I determined to come up with a more personal approach. This interactive resource is excellent for anyone dealing with the profound issues of death and loss through the restorative power of expressing true feelings no matter how unsettling. If we move too quickly or try to leap ahead, we end up right back where we don't want to be. If that takes one year, two, five, then we shouldn't have to explain or make excuses. Saying Goodbye to Chuck is an excellent method of incorporating a daily journal helping readers enunciate their own very personal grief process. I can't emphasize enough how helpful it is to document one's experience. A journal becomes your secret sanctuary, your most trusted confidante, and the friend to which you reveal your deepest truth. This book suggests accessible ways to write, to journal, and then to use that as a guide to the future. Together our experiences weave a tapestry displaying this universal truth at the heart of the human family, we are all one.

Lynne Zotalis is an award winning author placing 1st in the creative nonfiction category from Firebird Book Awards for Hippie at Heart (What I Used To Be, I Still Am). Her short stories have won publication for three years in the R.H. Cunningham Short Story Contest through Willowdown Books. Her poetry has appeared in Nature 20/20, Tuck Magazine, writinginawoman'svoice, The Poetic Bond VII, VIII and IX, and Lyrical Iowa. Saying Goodbye to Chuck, a daily journal helping to enunciate the readers' personal grief process along with her other publications are available on Amazon.

https://www.amazon.com/dp/B08DC6GZ7T

Ms. Zotalis' voice is honest, willing to take risks, which in my opinion, makes for a good book.
Julia Fricke Robinson, author of *All I Know.*

I am very impressed with Ms. Zotalis' quality and diversity of the style and subject, and how this overall collection feels -
the reflective poetry on human connections, love and life are powerful in Mysterious Existence.

Trevor Maynard, author and publisher of the ten volume series, *The Poetic Bond,* as well as *Paradox, Dark Sun Grey Moon* and *Keep on Keepin' On.*

www.ingramcontent.com/pod-product-compliance
Lightning Source LLC
Chambersburg PA
CBHW042125080426
42734CB00001B/4